Serial Killers
True Crime

Chilling True Crime Cases Of

The Worlds Most Twisted

Serial Killers And Criminals

Table of Contents

Do You Want More Books?

How would you like books arriving in your inbox each week?

Don't worry they are FREE!

We publish books on all sorts of non-fiction niches and send them out to our subscribers each week to spread the love.

All you have to do is sign up and you're good to go!

Just go to the link at the end of this book, sign up, sit back and wait for your book downloads to arrive!

We couldn't have made it any easier! Enjoy!

Introduction

I want to thank you and congratulate you for purchasing the book, *"Serial Killers True Crime: Chilling True Crime Cases Of The Worlds Most Twisted Serial Killers"*.

A lot of people have hobbies - most of the time, that hobby is directed by their penchant for a certain thing; sometimes travel and exploration, sometimes food, and in other cases, crafts.

However, there are people whose hobbies consist of sinister things: some of them desire to kill women, both young and old, children, or homosexuals. In this book, you will learn of 5 people whose desire to murder was sated – learn how they started, why did they did it, and how they were captured.

Thanks again for purchasing this book, I hope you enjoy it!

Chapter 1: The Darkness in Robert

Crimes, from small to large, often tend to disturb the public and place the police on high alert; but when the victims of these offenses are children, the people and law enforcers take an even greater interest - the perpetrator should be captured and should never be forgiven.

One such criminal was Robert Black, a Scottish pedophile who was at large for many years, leaving at least 4 children raped and murdered. A video documentary about Robert described him as "every parent's nightmare" and someone who was so full of psychopathy that he had no ability to feel remorse or empathy for his victims.

For him, these young girls were merely the expression of his pedophiliac desires.

Susan Never Returned

One hot Friday afternoon in July of 1982, in a peaceful farmhouse in Tweed, a small town on the English side of the English-Scottish border, 11 year old Susan Maxwell asked her mother, Liz, if she could cycle her way to the tennis court where she would play a game with another friend.

The tennis court was on the Scottish border, in Coldstream, which was 2 miles away from their home. At first, Liz was hesitant because of the traffic, but later on, she agreed, on the condition that Susan would walk. The mother figured that, although it would be Susan's first time to walk without adult supervision, there would no danger.

The route she would take was familiar, and the people were caring - they tended to look out for one another, especially for young children. Besides that, Susan should start learning how to go from one place to another on her own, so this could be her first lesson.

So off went Susan, but she didn't walk - a farmer, who was an acquaintance of the Maxwell family, was also going to Coldstream, so he offered to take Susan there. The girl, upon arriving at the court, played with Alison Raeburn, and all went according to plan.

Except for the fact that Susan never made it back home.

At around 4:00 pm, Liz decided that she would pick her daughter up; the weather was hot and Susan was probably too tired to walk home. While on her way, Liz wasn't expecting to actually reach the Lennel Tennis Club where her daughter played; she thought that she would encounter her daughter trudging in the opposite direction.

She thought she would just have to drive slowly and look for pedestrians. However, she didn't see Susan - not on the way to the court, and certainly not on the way back to the farm. When Liz called Alison, the child confirmed that she had left Susan making her walk home.

Liz panicked and called her husband, Fordyce, who instructed her to call the police immediately.

When the police began their investigation, they found out that Susan was seen numerous times from the time she had left the tennis court. Those who knew her personally and those who just remembered seeing a yellow dress-clad girl walking, while swinging a tennis racket, reported that she reached the Tweed Bridge safely.

But after that, the track went cold. No one witnessed when she was abducted, for if they did, they would have stopped the criminal.

It was horrifying, to say the least; the area where the Maxwells lived, the route to the tennis court, and even Coldstream, were all peaceful areas where crime virtually didn't happen. The disappearance of one girl was enough to disturb the residents.

Each day for the next two weeks, the Maxwells would be occupied. Fordyce headed out daily with other volunteer searchers, the number of which soon reached 2/3's of the Cornhill population, and Liz would update the press - it was vital to bring their daughter into the public eye as much as possible.

On August Friday the 13th of the same year, while doing an interview with *Radio 2*, the Maxwell parents were called by the police: the officer told them that they had found a little girl, but she "was not alive".

Just as the officer had been too polite not to mention the word "dead", he also calmly told the Liz and Fordyce, after their request to see the body, that the weather had been very warm for the past two weeks, and so, the body had decomposed badly.

So much so that visual identification would be impossible. The only way they were able to verify that it was indeed Susan, was from her dental records. Police reports indicated that the remains were discovered 250 miles away from the Tweed Bridge, in a ditch near the A518 Road in Loxley, just outside Uttoxeter in Midlands Staffordshire.

Since the body was found in Staffordshire, the police department there became the one responsible for the hunt for the killer. They interviewed more than 20,000 people, including witnesses of Susan's "final walk", people who were in the area where she was discovered, hotel staffs in case the perpetrator was a visitor, and truck drivers.

Despite the amount of information they gathered, there were no leads. The fact that the clues were not fed into a computer system was hard enough, but it was even harder to accept that although more than 500,000 index cards were in police custody - all pertaining to the Susan Maxwell Case - none of them became vital to the investigation.

It would take another murder for the police to have more information.

At the Fun City

On July 8, 1983, almost a year after Susan Maxwell had been abducted and murdered, 5 year old Caroline Hogg disappeared. Caroline's activities on that day were simple enough. She would have fun at a friend's afternoon party, then they would have dinner at home, and lastly, she would be seeing her grandmother to the bus stop. In all these "adventures", Annette, her mother, would be accompanying her.

However, after bidding goodbye to her grandmother, Caroline still had a lot of energy, so when they arrived at their home in Portobello at around 7 pm, she begged her mother to let her play down the road, in the playground which was just a short walk from their house. Annette agreed, but just for 5 minutes - so off went little Caroline to have the fun she wanted before bedtime.

When the time was up, Annette sent Stuart, her son, to bring his little sister home, but he couldn't find her. Annette headed out and when she couldn't find her either, the whole family searched for the energetic girl. By 8:00 pm, the police were already informed that Caroline Hogg was missing.

The starting point of the investigation was the playground where Caroline had played. Witnesses reported that while playing, a "scruffy man" was seen looking at the 5 year old, some moments later, the said man was seen holding hands with Caroline and they were headed to Fun City, a place where the girl wasn't allowed to go to. The last sighting was of the couple going out the back entrance of the amusement park.

It was Friday evening when Caroline went missing; on Sunday, more than 600 volunteers were helping in the search, and a week later, around 2,000 volunteers combed almost the entirety of Portobello. Annette and John Hogg talked to the media only once and in that moment, the two of them cried and begged for the safe return of their daughter.

Their efforts, however, were futile, because like Susan, the 5 year old was transported miles away from her home.

On July 18, 10 days after the disappearance, Caroline's body was discovered in Twycross, Leicestershire. It was an area which was 300 miles away from their home, but only 24 miles from where Susan Maxwell was found.

Like Susan's, Caroline's remains were also badly decomposed; the only identification was her locket and hairband. What made it worse for the Hogg family was the fact that their daughter's body was found naked - an indication that she had been sexually assaulted.

A Serial Killer on the Loose

The similarities in the Susan Maxwell and Caroline Hogg cases prompted the police to suspect that there was a serial killer on the loose; they had to act fast because if not, another young girl would turn up missing, and then, dead.

4 police departments merged for the capture of the killer: the Northumbria (where Susan was abducted), Staffordshire (where Susan's body was recovered), Edinburgh (where Caroline went missing), and Leicestershire (where Caroline was found).

In their search for answers, they realized that it would be so much better for the information and clues to be fed into a computer system, so in July of 1983, Hector Clark, the Deputy Chief Constable of the Northumbria Police, took charge of not just the investigation, but also of the computerization of the data.

The problem was, Susan's case alone had so many leads that it would be too time consuming, so after a thorough deliberation, they decided to computerize Caroline's case, and leave Susan's information for now.

As with the previous case, the investigation was massive; they interviewed thousands of people, inspected hotels, truck drivers, holidaymakers, and even staged a reconstruction of Caroline's last journey, but no amount of effort led them to the killer.

The police stayed vigilant, and for three years, the young girls of England remained safe, until March 26, 1986, when Sarah Harper went missing.

Into the Snicket and Gone

10 year old Sarah Harper lived with her family in Brunswick Place in Morley, Leeds, North of England, but slightly south from where Susan and Caroline resided. On

26th of March 1986, at around 8:00 pm, Sarah volunteered to buy a loaf of bread for her mother, Jacki.

The 10 year old took the £1 for the bread and a couple of lemonade bottles to get the deposit on them before heading out to *K&M Stores* at Peel Street, which was merely 100 yards away from Brunswick Place.

Mrs. Champaneri, the proprietor of *K&M*, reported that Sarah indeed went to the store, returned the bottles, and bought one loaf of white bread and 2 packets of crisps. On her way home, two other people saw her: they told the police that Sarah was entering the "snicket", an alley commonly used by locals as a shortcut. After that, Sarah Harper, 10 years old, disappeared.

It was 8:15 pm when Jacki decided to send one of her children to look for Sarah, who she suspected was eating crisps in the alley instead of coming straight home. When her daughter returned saying that Sarah was nowhere to be found, Jacki and other family members drove their car around the neighborhood hoping to find the girl.

When 9 o'clock came and Sarah was still missing, the family decided to call the police. Just like Susan's and Caroline's cases, the efforts had been extensive, but fruitless, for on April 19, more than 3 weeks after the disappearance, David Moult, a resident in Nottingham, discovered Sarah's body floating in the River Trent.

Reports said that the pre-mortem injuries were "terrible"; that the murderer, whoever he was, "explored" Sarah's vagina and anus.

Once all the information were in, Hector Clark believed that Sarah's murder was not connected to Susan's and Caroline's; according to him, the differences were so similarities could almost be ignored.

First, Susan and Caroline were kidnapped in a summer season, while wearing colorful clothes - Sarah was abducted on a rainy night, while wearing an anorak.

Second, Cornhill and Portobello were places near roads and were often traveled by people - Morley was the sort of place you would only visit for a particular reason.

Despite his conclusion, Hector Clark still kept an open mind, that maybe, although it was unlikely, the same killer did this to Sarah. According to the police, all the victims were young girls, taken from a public place, brought south to be sexually assaulted and murdered, and their remains were found within 26 miles of each other.

It was true that Sarah's murder was more brutal, but it could only mean that the serial killer was getting braver. Experts explained that as they become accustomed to their crimes, they would need more violence to fulfill their desires.

If that was the case, then the next attack would be more horrifying.

Fear and anger drove the police to be more aggressive - they had to end it once and for all. They used the Home Office Large Major Inquiry System or HOLMES: a system which had the ability to process, collate, and compare data to determine if one piece of information (name, plate number, address, etc.), had already turned up in another investigation at just the switch of a button.

However, the disadvantage of it was that if the name of the killer was not fed into the system, then, it wouldn't be able to pinpoint the perpetrator. It meant that they had to widen their scope.

So, even though Sarah's case was investigated separately from Susan's and Caroline's, the three were still linked. Her Majesty's Inspector of Constabulary commanded that the three cases should be placed into a single system; it was a gigantic task, the police knew, but because lives were at stake, they did what was necessary.

After three years of computerization, on July 1990, the database for the three brutal murders was completed. The only hurdle they needed to face was the effectiveness of this new database, and as sad as it sounded, Hector Clark knew that the best way they could catch the killer was if he would strike again.

"My biggest hope was that he would be caught before he went too far and killed another girl," he said.

Hector's hope, would be granted.

One Final Crime

On July 14, 1990, 6 year old Mandy Wilson was walking towards her friend's house in Stow, a village in the Scottish Borders, when she approached a van with the passenger door open. Fortunately, one neighbor, David Herkes, witnessed what happened. In his report, he said that he was bending low to check his mower blades when he saw Mandy's little feet besides those of a man.

David also witnessed the said man in the act of "stuffing" something under the dashboard, and then as quick as a lightning, the van drove towards Edinburgh. With great presence of mind, David memorized the car's registration number and immediately reported the incidence to the police, who responded quickly as did Mandy's father. As they stood near the spot where the girl was kidnapped, David saw the van again, and alerted the officers whom he had been reporting too.

Quickly, the police were able to capture Robert Black, and were able to save Mandy, who appeared to have already been sexually assaulted, but otherwise, safe.

Robert Black

Who was this man and why did he develop the need to assault girls and kill them?

From the records, Robert Black was born at Grangemouth (20 miles of Edinburgh) on April 21, 1947 to a woman named Jessie Hunter Black. His father was unknown, as Jessie refused to give the name of the man (the "Father" section of the birth certificate was left blank), but truthfully, even she was an estranged mother - leaving Robert virtually with no parents.

When Robert reached 6 months old, he was fostered out. Jessie was just 24, a woman who tried to make both ends meet with her little salary as a factory worker, but on top of that, she was unmarried - a social stigma during that time.

Within a year of giving Robert away, Jessie married a man named Francis Hall. In their life as a couple, they would have 4 children, but not one would know of a half-brother until said he made a name for himself (and not in a good way).

The family migrated to Australia, where Jessie died in 1982. Not once did she try to contact Robert, in fact, her family seemed to recall that she hated it to be known that she had a child out of wedlock.

While Jessie had what seemed to be a good life, Robert was being raised by Jack and Margaret Tulip, a couple who were in their fifties and who already had several experiences in taking foster kids. When Robert turned five, however, Jack died, leaving him totally under the care of Margaret.

Surprisingly, when the serial killer was interviewed after his capture, he confessed to Ray Wyre, a psychologist, that he had no recollection of his life before reaching 5 years old. Ray suggested that it was a common occurrence, but *only* to people who wanted to block out certain memories; after all, most of us would remember a piece of ourselves and how we were under the age of 5.

To emphasize this theory, the killer's neighbors conceded that Robert used to exhibit various injuries, although when asked about it, he didn't know how he got them. It was an indication that a form of physical abuse happened (perhaps, at Jack's hands), but Robert didn't want to remember it.

Under Margaret's care, Robert didn't recall any serious

abuse, but he remembered those times when his foster mother would lock him up, or hit him with a belt for unruly behavior. In school, Robert was a bully; his classmates reported that he chose to hang out with kids a few years younger than he was, probably because he could easily dominate them with his age and physical advantage.

Sometimes, Robert would exhibit "sudden, mindless violence," when, out of nowhere, he would pick a target (usually weak and younger), and would beat him up for no reason at all.

These tendencies continued and Robert became infamous as a wild boy. Someone who had no respect for authorities, who didn't care about anyone, and who would bully his way around just because he wanted to but he was never be involved in anything more serious.

That didn't mean that he had no secrets.

During his arrest in 1990, Robert became vocal about his childhood fantasies. At the age of 8, he began his sexual exploration in the form of inserting various things into his anus; and because he was somewhat in awe about it, he took pictures, which of course, were shown to the police.

The objects he would insert in his anus varied from a simple pen to a table leg; Robert apparently wanted to know "how much" he could take in.

The serial killer also disclosed that he was bothered with the feeling that perhaps, he wanted to be a girl - to be more specific, he wanted to have a vagina instead of a penis. However, nothing in his demeanor was feminine; through the years he had numerous sexual experiences with girls and he claimed to have liked each one of them.

Psychologists explained that perhaps, the reason for his desire to explore what's within him (anus), and his fascination for a vagina, were brought about by his lack of identity; a person who had never met his birth mother could be tempted to explore his deepest, darkest secrets.

The Final Straw

It was when his second mother, Margaret Tulip, died in 1958 that Robert's behavior turned from nasty to criminal - he was just 12 years old and had been transferred to Redding Children's Home. Whilst here he and two other friends, tried to rape a girl. After the incident had been made known to the authorities, he was moved to Red House, an all-male facility with stricter disciplinary rules.

There, Robert was sexually abused by one of the male staff, but despite that, he excelled academically and was even accepted into Musselburgh Grammar School. Sports became his solace, especially football and swimming. He could have continued a career as a football player, but his eyesight problems proved to be a hard obstacle to beat.

Given this unfortunate scenario, he focused on swimming and later on worked as a lifeguard where his pedophiliac desires increased. In fact, in Portobello where Caroline Hogg was abducted, there were two swimming pools that Robert frequented.

When Robert turned 15, his time in the Red House was up, so the authorities helped him establish a life of his own by recommending a place for him to stay and by giving him a job as a delivery boy. It was in that job that he started molesting female customers.

He would ask permission to enter the house or flat, and then they would talk before he proceeded on touching them sexually - sometimes the customers relented, sometimes they didn't, but none of these harassments were reported.

Until a 17 year-old Robert tried to rape and kill a 7 year old girl. In his story, he lured the child from a park under the pretense of seeing some kittens. When they were alone, he strangled her to the point of unconsciousness before he poked a finger in her vagina.

While some rapists and killers get aroused with a struggling victim, Robert was fond of inert young girls, so although he didn't totally rape the girl, he masturbated above her passive body. After he was done, he went away as if nothing happened, not caring if the girl was dead or alive.

The Police, upon learning what had happened, only admonished Robert; warning him that he better be on his best behavior in the future. Psychiatrists who examined him even reported that the event was just an "isolated" case, and would not hamper his development as a growing adult.

Contradicting this conclusion, the Social Services who checked on him told the court that it was a serious matter, and that Robert should be sent back home to Grangemouth where he could start anew.

At first, the plan worked, he got a job and was even involved with a certain Pamela Hodgson, but after some time, the relationship, which, according to Robert was his first and last real commitment, ended. It wasn't clear why, but many speculated that Pamela might have heard of her boyfriend's offenses, or worse, she experienced it first hand.

In his interview later, Robert would imply that it was that breakup which forced his hand to murder. He said: "Tell Pamela she's not responsible for all this," which actually meant the opposite.

Seeking Justice

When Robert was arrested, Hector Clark knew that he was their man, but gut feelings were not enough - they had to prove it. They investigated his job as a van driver and found his routes, as well as gas station receipts which connected him to the three cases. These added to the fact that he had kidnapped and sexually assaulted Mandy Wilson.

He was sentenced to a lifetime in prison, and would need to serve 35 years behind bars before being eligible for parole.

It was worth noting that Robert denied all the charges despite the evidence.

Chapter 2: His Personal Graveyard

The 1970s in the United States was a time of worry, particularly about security. The years before that, several serial killers had been discovered - so the people's idea that their security was infallible was shattered. 2 years ago, the Manson Family perpetrated the Sharon Tate and La Bianca murders, then, Mack Ray Edwards admitted that since the 1950s, he had been killing children, and before that, in 1964, the Boston Strangler wreaked havoc.

The people were on high alert, and they weren't wrong to be so.

On May 19, 1971, a Japanese farmer named Goro Kagehiro inspected his orchard near the Feather River Five in Sutter County, California. On his tour, he noticed that there was a man-sized, freshly dug hole between two trees. It was weird-looking, according to Goro, but he continued making his tour.

Later that night, still feeling concerned, he went back to the orchard and was shocked to see that the hole was already filled up. Thinking that a trespasser was using his land as a dumping site, he called the police, who immediately proceeded to dig it up.

There was no trash, but there was a dead body of a white man.

The victim, Kenneth Whiteacre (a drifter), had been bashed on the head, stabbed in the chest, and slashed multiple times across the back of his head. Police concluded that a struggle had been involved, judging by the slashes present on his arms and hands. In his pocket, the authorities found literature which suggested that he was a homosexual.

That tidbit of information soothed their worries: yes, it was disturbing to find a dead body, but the odds were, it was just an isolated crime. Apparently, during that time, The Gay Right's movements were making some noise and people who found their lifestyle bothering tended to be hostile.

On that night, the police's only goal was to find a supposed "hate" killer, not a serial one - there was no need to alarm the public more than they already were.

But some people believed that the authorities slacked off in their investigation; for instance, they didn't search the body for evidence of sexual assault - once they learned that his head injuries were acquired post-mortem, they relinquished the remains to the mortician.

The only conclusion they offered was that the attack was made in anger (probably a hate crime). After that, they filed this case as unsolved, but random.

Until May 24 when some workers noticed that a portion of the land in the adjacent ranch had collapsed.

The foreman of the workers, Ray Duron, immediately called the police, thinking that it was connected to the previous hole dug up in the orchard, and true enough, when they searched, another dead body of a white man was discovered. This time, the victim was Charles Fleming, another homeless man.

Already alarmed because two cases with similar scenarios were no longer random, the police spent the whole day investigating the surrounding area. Their inspection was fruitless until one officer noticed that there was a "weedy area" near the peach orchard.

In that spot, they saw another land portion with subsidence, so for the second time that day, they dug again. Superficially, they found a receipt for a meat purchase in Yuba City -it bore the name Juan V. Corona. More digging and another body turned up.

The victim this time was not a drifter, but an indigent farmhand. Like the other two corpses, he had sustained head injuries from a sharp object, probably a machete.

Although no other clues were found in the surrounding areas, the name Juan V. Corona was more than enough to start a fruitful investigation.

A Suspect under Surveillance

The similarities in the cases suggested that the police had a serial killer on the loose. They shouldn't take it lightly because sooner or later, another body might turn up. Sheriff Roy Whiteaker began his analysis with the only name they had so far - Juan V. Corona.

The man under scrutiny was 37 years old, and he was currently a suspect for another offense. In Marysville across the Feather River, in a restaurant owned by his gay half-brother, Juan was suspected to have beaten a man named Jose Raya nearly to death.

Like the corpses the police had discovered, Jose Raya also had head injuries. Sheriff Roy suspected Juan for various reasons:

a) he was there the evening the beating took place,

b) he was known around the area as a homophobic person (to the point of rage),

c) he was said to have been confined to a mental institution during the 1950s due to schizophrenia, and

d) the blue-and-white pickup truck seen near the areas of digging was similar to Juan's vehicle.

When the Sutter County District Attorney, Dave Teja, learned of the "Graveyard Lane", he became excited - he wanted to handle a first-degree murder case, and now he had one. With Sheriff Roy, he discussed the possibility of arresting Juan Corona, but the Sheriff refused.

Arresting someone only on the basis of receipts would only get the police force in trouble - they needed more conclusive evidence. Sheriff Roy thought that if the killer was so careless that he dropped something out of his pockets and didn't notice it, then the chances that they could uncover more clues were high, they just needed to dig some more.

Many volunteers helped in the grave-searching. Some of them even wanted to see first hand what the big deal was, but many of those who assisted, both police and civilian volunteers, were unprepared for the number of bodies and their condition.

There were a total of 9 bodies found in that area alone- and they were at different stages of decomposition. Volunteers sometimes accidentally cut a body part with the sharp part of the shovel because the remains had already severely decomposed.

After the digging, the bodies would be lined up in the mortuary for clues, which became elusive until they identified them. Apparently, many of the victims were linked with Juan for some reason. Either they had talked to him at one point, or they were last seen together with him -the latter clue was more evident.

Albeit circumstantial, the police deemed it enough to obtain a search warrant for Juan's home, office, and car.

Cornered

On May 26, 1971, the police went to Juan Corona's house where he lived together with his wife and 4 daughters. After arresting him, they started the search. Inside their home, they found evidence which could physically link him to the murders like:

- a posthole digger,

could-be weapons such as:

- a stained wooden club,
- meat cleaver, and
- hatchet, and

bloodstained vehicles:

- Chevrolet Impala and

- a van - which contained things like: machete, bag of bullets, several clothes, and a shovel.

The police officers also noticed other meat receipts, and a ledger which enumerated names of men - some of which were victims.

Juan also had an office in the Sullivan Ranch, the area where the police discovered the second body. In the said office, they found a pistol and a knife which had the label: Tennessee Toothpick.

Considering all these clues, the police became bothered; what if Juan Corona was truly their man? And what if his ledger was a record of those he had killed? Then that meant they had to unearth more victims.

That, they did, and they were shocked to find almost twice as many bodies as the first batch of digging discovered; all in all, there were 25 bodies now.

Not surprisingly all the victims were either drifters or migrant workers, but there were none of Mexican decent. Their ages ranged from 40 to 68. Many of the bodies were recovered on the north side of a tree, with their hands above their head, as if they had been sacrificial lambs to a ritual slaughter.

Panic in Sutter County

At the news that more bodies had been recovered and that there could be more, the press and people who had lost someone started asking the police for more information. As much as they wanted to establish that all the victims were accounted for, they couldn't - they had to think not just of the relatives, but also of the victims; they all deserved to be laid to rest.

When the diggers discovered another hole that contained not a dead body but several deposit slips, they almost shouted Eureka! The deposit slips were again in the name of Juan Vallejo Corona.

Perhaps pressured by the press and the public, Sheriff Roy Whiteaker made the mistake of announcing in a conference that they had the man they believed to be the murderer. A lot of people believed it was an action uncalled for, because during that time, the evidence was still inconclusive and Juan still hadn't undergone trial.

Attorney Richard Hawk

While Juan was in jail, the authorities continued their search for more solid evidence. They also started putting Juan's background under the microscope. They established that he was a labor contractor, someone who provided workers to the ranch owners.

Although he tended to pay less for their labor, there was no report of abuse, in fact, those who took workers from him attested to the police that he was a good man. A solid family man and an avid churchgoer, those were Juan's general descriptions. A little interesting fact was that none of the laborers he had were white - all of them were Mexicans.

As he waited in vain, Juan didn't exhibit any form of madness as other serial killers usually did, one of the reporters even described him as depressed, but humble. When his defense was handed over to Attorney Richard Hawk, Juan saw some light. The aggressive defense lawyer came from Yuba City and he meant business.

His first actions were to fire the psychiatrists who made contradictory remarks (the examining psychiatrist said Juan was sane, while the prosecuting psychiatrist deemed him psychotic) and filing a lawsuit charge against Sheriff Roy and other county officials.

According to him, the police violated a number of Juan's rights, which resulted in slander and emotional depression. Despite the gag order, Attorney Hawk showed the ledger to some reporters, insisting that although half of the names were indeed victims, the experts from the police force couldn't even say directly that Juan had written them.

On top of that, the "blood evidence" was contested because examinations showed that it was actually animal blood or paint. Attorney Hawk also explained that the blood in Juan's vehicle came from one of his workers who was injured. In other words, aside from the receipts, there was no physical evidence to link Juan to any of the murders.

For instance, only one victim was found to have been killed using a machete, but when the authorities tested Juan's machete, there was no bloodstain, and a link to the actual wound was not established.

Even more bothering was the fact that the tire tracks didn't match any of Juan's vehicles and the bullet found in one of the victims didn't match his gun. The receipts were also contested because the experts were not able to prove that Juan was the only one who had touched them, nor could they prove that it was dropped there on the day the victim was buried.

Ultimately, Attorney Hawk argued that at the times the victims were supposed to have been attacked, Juan was on crutches.

All in all, Attorney Richard Hawk knew that the evidence

was not enough, but he also knew that cases like this one tended to be a lump in the throat - if the jury wanted it to be closed once and for all, they might convict Juan, weak evidence or not.

So, he did his best to gain favors for himself and his client - he encouraged the trial to be held elsewhere (in Fairfield) because he felt Jual wouldn't get a fair trial in Sutter County. He also acquired media connections to encourage the public to think that someone else had framed his client. Attorney Hawk even used Jose Raya's case, informing everyone that it was Natividad Corona, Juan's brother, who should be convicted and not Juan.

The Battle

The trial began on September 11, 1972, and a lot of people remembered it as being chaotic as many "mistakes" had been made. The prosecuting attorney, Dave Teja, for example, failed to get the blood on the knife tested, and he scrambled to have it done at the last minute.

The results? It didn't match any of the victims, not even Juan Corona. Another mistake was the tire tracks - the police found out later that the cast used to compare the track to Juan's vehicle came from another case - someone had mixed them up during the investigation.

While Attorney Richard Hawk provided the jury with countless counter-attacks to the prosecution's evidence (primarily implying that the real killer was Natividad Corona), Attorney Dave Teja failed to submit a number of reports, angering the judges.

One of the pieces of evidence was a cigarette with a trace of saliva. Initially, the experts said it didn't match any of the victims or Corona's but later on, they changed their statement, telling the judges that there had been a mistake when they collected Juan's saliva which they used for comparison.

Although Hawk used it against the prosecution, implying that they were deliberately sabotaging the clues, he too, was admonished for not being able to produce the laborers from whom the blood in Juan's vehicle came from. Dave Teja's team said that the blood seemed to have three types, strange because it meant three laborers were injured – an unlikely scenario.

The court became a battle ground between Richard Hawk and Dave Teja, but soon, when Attorney Dave was replaced by another, more experienced attorney, Ronald Fahey, it became personal. It seemed like the two lawyers were not keen on finding the truth, instead, they were determined to prove that the other was wrong.

In other words, the trial became a messy procedure - nothing was neat or organized.

In their last argument, Richard Hawk demanded that Juan Corona should be acquitted because there was virtually no evidence to link him to the murders, but when the jury denied his demand, he told the court that he "rests his case". This was very surprising, considering that he had been very adamant all throughout the proceedings.

Convicting Corona

In the end, the judges favored the prosecution; many believed that Richard made a huge mistake in resting the case without calling out witnesses, not even Juan himself. The decision (25 life terms in prison), was appealed but after the second trial, it was reinstated, especially since during his imprisonment, Juan Corona was rumored to have confessed to a priest and fellow inmates.

He told them that he did it, but that he shouldn't be judged because he was sick, and sick men should not attend the trial of normal people.

Those who were not officially included in the investigation, but were avid followers, believed that Juan was the killer, and that Richard Hawk should have explored the possibility of insanity instead of "showing off".

Chapter 3: Bela and His Pickled Women

Most serial killers are convicted; a lot of times the process of identifying him (or her), is long and hard, but in the end, they are sentenced to prison, or sometimes, death. There however are a number of instances where the police force have not been able to pinpoint who the killer was, such as in the case of the Zodiac Killer.

It could be that he had had his fill of killings and he stopped purposely, or that he had died due to some reason. It's very strange to have a serial killer, identify him, but not put him behind bars - because he vanished and left no trace.

A Simple, but Well-Liked Man

Bela Kiss was born in 1877 in Hungary, and he grew up to be a fine man. In the 1900s, he moved to 9 Kossuth Street near Cinkota, a town outside Budapest (although now, Czinkota is already a town within Budapest). A handsome young man with blond hair and appealing blue eyes, Bela earned a living as a tinsmith, but his hobbies signified depth of character.

According to reports, he was an amateur astrologer, a voracious reader who indulged in history and literature, and an avid art lover. Even though he lacked a formal education, any conversation with Bela was intelligent.

Although not a wealthy man, Bela was well-liked, especially by the women; he threw parties at local hotels and he was generous. Despite all these good things, he was an established paradox.

He didn't seem like a man who wanted to tie the knot, but he kept on entertaining women, even to the point of renting a hotel in Budapest (because choices of female companions in Cinkota were limited) and posting advertisements in newspapers, which of course, always received favorable responses.

Because he had no wife to tend to him, Bela hired Mrs. John Jakubec in 1912 to take care of the household chores. Reports said that Mrs. Jakubec found it strange that even though there was a steady stream of female companions in Bela's house, she didn't get the chance to meet any of them. It seemed like as quick as they came, the women were also quick to go.

Another strange thing about Bela was his sudden need to purchase a number of huge metal drums. The strangeness of this caught the attention of the townspeople so that they even involved the police. When questioned, Bela confidently replied that he would use the drums to store oil for the upcoming war.

In 1914, when Bela was already 34 years old, World War 1 broke out so, he left his house as a soldier, leaving everything in the hands of Mrs. Jakubec.

An Appalling Surprise

On July of 1916, Dr. Charles Nagy, the Chief Detective of Budapest Police, received a frantic call. A landlord in Cinkota feared that he had found evidence of murder at his property. In his report, the landlord said that his tenant, a soldier named Bela Kiss, failed to pay for the lease of the house in Kossuth Street.

Rumors had it that he could be a prisoner of war, or perhaps, he had died in battle. Thinking that he needed to rent out the house to another person, he went to the house to inspect it and see what repairs were needed. Upon his arrival, he noticed that there were some huge drums just outside the house.

When he poked one of them, he smelled something so awful that he called a chemist who was living near the area. The chemist confirmed that the smell could only come from a decomposing human body.

Dr. Nagy, together with two other detectives, ventured to Cinkota, but when they reached Kossuth, they were greeted not only by a worried landlord, but also by an irate Mrs. Jakubec, who was demanding that they leave her master's house alone.

Ignoring the old housekeeper, Dr. Nagy and the detectives proceeded to inspect the drum, and when they opened it, their worst fears were confirmed. The drum was filled with wood alcohol, and the sack in it contained the body of a young woman with black-brown hair.

Judging by the rope found along with the remains, it was clear that the woman had died due to strangulation. 6 other drums were opened and all of them contained a young woman's naked body - all had been strangled.

It seemed like Bela was trying to preserve the bodies - just like how pickles are produced. Dr. Nagy's initial action was to interrogate Mrs. Jakubec. According to her, the huge metal containers had been an issue before because people thought that Bela would be storing illegally acquired liquors.

When the soldier assured that he would just be filling it with gasoline to prepare for the war, the issues died down.

Obviously, Bela lied.

Afraid that there were more secrets in 9 Kossuth Street, the officers inspected the ground around the house. They were not mistaken, other bodies were unearthed and they too, had been preserved using wood alcohol. The preservation was so good that the physical features of the ladies could still be recognized, making the identification process easy for the police.

Call to Action

Dr. Charles Nagy was not a novice - he had been on the Force for quite some time, but he admitted to having no experience with a case such as that in 9 Kossuth Street. Afraid that he might commit a major mistake, he immediately alerted everyone concerned.

First, he sent a message to the military department - if Bela Kiss was still on the front line, then he was to be arrested immediately. Next, he commanded all the telegraph and postal services that they should intercept any letter either sent or received by Bela Kiss, in case the soldier had an accomplice.

Lastly, he detained the terrified housekeeper, determined to get as much information from her as possible. The only problem now was capturing Bela Kiss. A task which proved to be more difficult than expected.

During that time, thousands of Hungarian soldiers were imprisoned, and the army itself was scattered because of the war. What made the search worse was Bela's name: Bela Kiss was a really common name and without the presence of a photograph (they only used sketches), identifying the serial killer was a herculean task.

With nothing more to do about hunting the murderer, Dr. Nagy focused on the victims and the scared Mrs. Jakubec, who insisted that she knew nothing of the terrible crimes. She reiterated that Bela Kiss was just a man who treated her well, and who provided her with a good wage.

As if to prove her innocence, the housekeeper took the officers around the house, starting with Bela's room. As they continued the tour inside the house, Dr. Nagy noticed another room with a locked door.

Mrs. Jakubec explained that it was the "secret room", and that her master had told her that she was not allowed to enter it - no one except Bela Kiss himself was allowed inside the locked room.

Seeing that the rules no longer applied, the housekeeper provided Dr. Nagy with the key to the secret abode. Upon their entrance, nothing seemed amiss: the room was just filled with books (not strange because Bela was a known reader), and the only furniture aside from the bookcases were a desk and a chair.

In the drawers of the desk, Dr, Nagy found letters between Bela and the women he had been with - there were also photographs of hundreds of ladies.

The letters were organized in such a way that all the letters coming from one sender were kept in a single file - there were 74 files in total, signifying 74 women. A hundred other letters which were not organized seemed to mean that Bela wasn't interested in them.

Apparently, the letters were the different women's response to the ads Bela had posted and all of them had been interested in marriage. Surprisingly, to the 74 women he had corresponded with, he agreed to marry them.

Even more shocking was the fact that Bela seemed to have taken money from the women he'd been with. Some of the instances were so severe that the woman was robbed of her entire bank savings.

Finding the letters a little too taxing, he analyzed the books, and was bewildered to realize that most of them were about creating poisons and performing strangulations. If the clues found in the secret room were to be considered, Dr. Nagy was worried that more bodies would turn up.

Bela Kiss According to His Housekeeper

Now fully aware of her master's morbid imperfections, Mrs. Jacubek began spilling out what she knew about Bela Kiss, but not in an attempt to persecute him, but to insist that someone else had framed him. According to her, Bela arrived in Cinkota in 1890, when he was just 23 years old.

More than just good-looking, the young man had been polite. Everyone in the neighborhood liked him, and not once did he hurt anyone, in fact, he was caring, even to the animals. She cited one instance when an injured dog came into the area - Bela didn't hesitate to nurse it back to health.

As for his penchant with women, she confided that her master was indeed a lady's man. Many women would be welcomed into the house, but not once did she know of their names. She didn't even speak to them unless it was to follow an order.

According to Mrs. Jacubek, most of the girls were city-bred, and not peasants like her, hence, she didn't find it her place to intrude.

Despite the fact that the housekeeper seemed sincerely

innocent, Dr. Nagy didn't let her out off the hook yet, especially when he found out how "substantially" Bela had been paying her.

However, since it was obvious that she was fearful of being put into prison, they took a break in the interrogation. The officers began investigating who Bela was according to his neighbors.

And sadly (for Dr. Nagy), their comments were the same as the ones provided by the housekeeper. Bela was a fine young man, and it wasn't surprising to see him with a couple of ladies because of his looks and polite, intelligent attitude.

Understanding His Psyche

Getting deeper into their investigation, the police department in Cinkota were able to understand how Bela Kiss lured his victims. With his amiable character and above average reputation, his newspaper ads became a hit. When a woman started corresponding with him, he would then ask about her financial status.

If he was satisfied, the next step would be to spoil the prospective victim - but not before learning that she had no close relatives. It meant that should he dispose of the lady, then no one would come looking for her.

Dr. Nagy was also surprised to learn that most women were prepared to send Bela a lot of money, sometimes, to the point that their entire savings were used. If, by any chance, Bela had already gotten everything and he no longer appeared interested in her, the correspondence would stop.

If the woman dared or gave an inkling of calling the police, she would be killed.

One of his victims was Katherine Varga (identified so because of the K.V. initials in her clothing), a dress shop owner and a widow from Budapest. Katherine was still young, and her business was doing well. The fact that she had no relatives also made her perfect for Bela Kiss.

Once the "wedding" was finalized, she sold her business and apparently gave all the money to Bela, who in turn, killed her. Two similar occasions were of Julia Paschak and Elizabeth Komeromi; the two apparently gave a lot of money to Bela on the pretense that they were to be married, but when they didn't, the women sued the tinsmith.

However, since the two women didn't appear before the court, the lawsuit was dropped.

Then, more evidence appeared in the person of Mrs.

Stephen Toth. Mrs. Toth told the police officers that she came to Cinkota to look for a man named Bela Kiss, someone she was introduced to by her daughter, Margaret. According to her story, Margaret came to Budapest to work, and one day, she announced that she would be marrying Bela Kiss.

The man asked for money for the upcoming marriage and the supportive mother provided it, however, when no marriage happened, and Mrs. Stephen accused Bela of reneging on the wedding, he told her that it was just delayed, and that it was Margaret who had left for America.

There was even a letter from Margaret to prove the departure - she told her mother that Bela's rejection was too much for her, and so, she would be finding her new love in America.

Dr. Nagy found out that it was just a ruse; before Bela strangled Margaret to death, he forced her to write the misleading letter to her mother.

Margaret, Julia, Elizabeth, and Katherine were just 4 victims, buy if the clues left by Bela were anything to go by, his victims could reach up to 30 women - the police needed to capture him fast.

The Hunt for Bela Kiss

After everyone in the military had been informed of what happened, the search was intensified. No killer should be spared, especially not Bela whose manner of deceit and murder was premeditated and whose victims could number as high as 30.

On October 4, 1916, Dr. Nagy received intelligence that Bela Kiss had died of typhoid in 1915, but soon afterwards, it was retracted. It was found that Bela was alive and he was confined to an Hungarian hospital. Overwhelmed, his team didn't waste a moment, they went straight to the hospital; however, they were shocked to discover that the man in Bela Kiss' bed was dead, and it was not the soldier they were looking for.

The initial reaction of course, was to think that Bela somehow knew of the upcoming arrest, and he had switched the body, so Dr. Nagy sent out word telling the entire police and military force that Bela had escaped.

But he was never captured. Throughout the years, rumor after rumor would reach the authorities - some indicated that Bela was at a certain place, living someone else's life - other reports said he had died of a disease.

The difficulty of the matter was not fully knowing how many women had been killed, and accepting that no justice would be served for the known victims.

Chapter 4: Ire with Older Women

The Dark Strangler, the Gorilla Killer, these were the names assigned to Earle Nelson - perhaps one of the most prolific serial killers in the history of the United States. Unlike other murderers, Earle seldom used a weapon - there was no fun in it - his victims needed to die in his hands, literally, by strangling the life out of them.

People thought him to be inhuman; not only because of the murders, but because of how he was able to perform them: sneaking in and out in populous areas without scaring someone off seemed to be an extraordinary talent.

A Serial Killer in the Making

Just like most serial killers, Earle Nelson had a troubled childhood: both his parents died when he was still an infant. His mother, Frances Nelson, died of syphilis when Earle was just 9 months old, soon after, his father's demise occurred.

The only thing the man left him was the surname Ferall (meaning Wild), but Earle would also relinquish it once he was transferred to San Francisco, into the care of his maternal grandmother, who was a widow and had 2 children of her own to raise.

Experts suggest that the presence of a dominant female figure was a common occurrence in the life of future killers, but Earle's grandmother truly cared for him, it was just that she was overworked from raising three kids. Worse, Earle proved to be a difficult child.

He had no manners when it came to hygiene (no matter how much his grandmother insisted on it) and at times he appeared hyperactive, and then at others, depressed.

Worse, the people in the household (his aunt and uncle, the siblings of his mother), always made fun of his peculiar behaviors. Harold Schechter, a biographer, wrote in his book entitled *Bestial*, an instance when Earle poured olive oil on his food before plunging his face onto the plate, ravaging the meal as if he was a feral animal.

Due to this, the children took to calling him an "animal". Another example was how Earle would go home from school wearing a different set of filthy clothes when he was sent away wearing clean ones.

His fondness for the Holy Bible was also contradictory to his wild behavior. In Grade 7, he was expelled from school because he was "incorrigible"; his loneliness and quietness as a child was negated by his violence when provoked. On more than one occasion, Earle was also caught stealing various, trivial items from a shop.

When he was 11 years old, Earle was involved in a bicycle accident which caused him a serious head injury. According to reports, for almost a week after the accident, Earle suffered from both unconsciousness and delirium. But after he was out of the woods, his health remained intact.

Time and time again, Earle failed to meet the expectations of his grandmother, especially in the area of religion. While the old woman was a devout Pentecostal, Earle grew up to be a reckless, young man - far from the God-fearing person he was expected to be.

No one knew for certain if his head injury might have contributed to his desire to kill, but that desire was fulfilled.

Fallen Sanity

When Earle turned 14 years old, his grandmother died, leaving him in the care of his aunt Lillian, and her husband. At that time, Lillian was only 24, and already, she was left with the responsibility of raising a teenage drop out. Despite this, she stood by Earle (even after knowing his unforgivable crimes), because for her, family should be given the utmost attention.

Given her fondness for her nephew (although she admitted to having been afraid of him), Lillian tended to "ignore" his misdemeanors. He never went back to school, he moved onto doing menial jobs, and got fired due to laziness and strange behaviors. At work, Earle was often reprimanded for his slacking off.

When a task was assigned to him, it wouldn't be finished because he spent the working hours meandering about the work place. His odd behavior of returning home with different set of clothes also persisted, as well as his loneliness and temper.

At the age of 15, his sexual desires were already at their peak; he was a "voracious masturbator", and was a frequent visitor of prostitutes near the Fisherman's Wharf. On top of insatiable sexual needs, Earle also turned to alcoholism, and was able to develop a world of his own.

Reports said that he was daydreamer - he spent hours each day talking to invisible people and battling non-existent enemies; at times he even went home bruised and battered as if a real fight had ensued.

Days, weeks, and months, these faults would not improve,

if any, they seemed to worsen. In 1915, Earle began journeying; initially it would just be for a couple of days, but later on, he was absent for weeks and months.

Performing odd jobs and stealing became his primary ways of financing his penchant for traveling. These burglaries also became his ticket to jail. One time, he rummaged through what he thought was an empty cabin, but while getting away, the owner showed up, surprising him. Once caught red-handed, he was tried, and convicted of burglary - the punishment was 2 years in San Quentin Prison.

Once released, Earle decided to enlist in the US Army under the name Earle Leonard Ferral (his father's surname), but just as he had slacked off on his previous jobs, Earle also went AWOL and headed to Salt Lake City, Utah. There, he became a Mormon, but that too, didn't last.

After this, as if he hadn't already proven that he wasn't cut out for military work, he enlisted in the US Navy, where he was assigned to be a cook. A little over a month after being accepted, he left the job, siting that the tasks were burdensome.

His life became more wayward than before: he traveled around the Bay Area for months before deciding to work as a medical corpsman which only exacerbated his mental deterioration. His attempt to go back to the navy was disastrous - he refused to work, instead, he spent time reading the Bible and discussing the Apocalypse.

Clearly, he was suffering psychologically so he was admitted to Napa State Mental Hospital, where he escaped twice, and was also captured twice, earning the name "Houdini". On the third time he escaped, the medical staff didn't even bother to search for him - they just removed his name from the enlisted personnel, and proclaimed him as being "improved," "non-violent, homicidal, or destructive."

Earle as a Married Man

An escapee from the mental institution, Earle went back to his Aunt Lillian, who welcomed him back with open arms. Not only did her family provide for Earle once more, but they also helped him get another janitorial job in a hospital near San Francisco.

It was here the soon-to-be serial killer met Mary Martin, a 58 year old housekeeper and an old maid. In his interviews, Earle said that he was attracted to Mary's maternal instinct, so very much like her grandmother's. Not even knowing each other that well, the couple married in 1919, in Mary's religion, Catholicism.

As soon as the two moved in together, Mary realized that they had different goals in mind. While she wanted to have an equal partnership, Earle apparently wanted to "role play"- she was supposed to be the caring mother, and he was the disobedient son. Mary discovered how trying Earle was.

How he changed from clean clothes to a different set of filthy ones, how he had an insatiable sexual desire, and how jealous he could be in the slightest sign that Mary was becoming "overly friendly" towards any male. And although he didn't hurt Mary, Earle always tended to pour his rage into inanimate objects.

Earle's descent into madness was accompanied by migraines and intermittent headaches which no medicine could cure, not even the genuine care he received from Mary lessened the pain. One time at work, the ache became so severe that Earle fell from a ladder, sustaining another head injury.

After this, he became even more violent and unstable, and for the first time, Mary became afraid of him. When Earle decided to leave Palo Alto, Mary refused to go with him so he left alone, but also returned a day later, begging her to take him back. The old woman had the sense to refuse, and that was when Earle literally lost it: his need to murder old women (like Mary and his grandmother) emerged.

First Attack

Reeling from Mary's rejection, Earle set out to claim his first victim. On May 19, 1921, Earle posing as a plumber, went to Charles Summers' home, and was invited in by 24 year old Charles Jr., the owner's son. Once there, he immediately went to the basement where 12 year old Mary Summers was playing.

Not wasting a moment, Earle attacked the child and strangled her. Fortunately, the young victim fought hard, scratching Earle anywhere she could reach him, kicking and screaming and calling for her brother, who immediately went to her rescue.

Earle was able to escape after delivering a stunning blow to the young Charles, but he was soon captured.

In the prison, his bizarre behavior alarmed his jail mates: one time he plucked all his eyebrows using just his fingers, and on more than one occasion, he shouted that there were faces on the wall. When Mary Martin, his wife, was informed of his husband's predicament, she went to the hospital and took care of him.

Despite being informed (for the first time) that her

husband had been admitted to a mental hospital, that he had been convicted before, and that he had been dismissed from the military, Mary stuck by him.

He was tried and examined, and in the end, the judges considered him a danger to "wife and self" and that with him at large could pose a danger to people. For the second time in his life, he was admitted to the Napa State Mental Hospital.

The first year of his stay in Napa was good: he showed signs of improvement, and even though his diagnosis was "nomadic dementia" and "constitutional psychopath with outbreaks of psychosis", the staff soon trusted him enough to go to certain places, unrestrained.

However, at around 18 months into his confinement, Earle became agitated, both depressed, and excited. On November of 1923, Earle successfully escaped the hospital and went home to his Aunt Lillian, who accepted him despite her fear for the safety of her family. According to her, after giving Earle some of her husband's clothes, she encouraged him to run away, telling him that he wasn't safe there.

Earle agreed and left. Lillian then immediately called the police and the Napa mental hospital to inform them that Earle had been to her house.

After a thorough search, Earle was captured and was again sent to Napa State Mental Hospital. 4 years after his attack on Mary Summers, he was discharged as "improved". Mary took him back, but after only a couple of weeks, his "nomadic dementia" struck again, so he traveled northwest and started his killing spree.

Attacks of the Dark Strangler

On February 20, 1926, Earle Nelson saw the "For Rent" sign in one of the houses in Pierce Street, San Francisco. Dressed in a clean suit, he appeared before the landlady, 62 year old Clara Newman, a widow. Impressed by his manners and his very clean appearance (as she was very "picky" when it came to accepting borders), Clara let Earle Nelson in, not thinking that in doing so, she had welcomed in her killer.

On the second floor of the house, Merton Newmann Sr., Clara's nephew, was feeling chilly. Thinking that the furnace in the basement was being difficult again, he went down to fix it. On his way, he saw that the sausages had been left on the stove; he figured that something must have interrupted his aunt in cooking, but there was nothing unusual about that, knowing that there were boarders around the house.

Walking toward the basement, he saw a large man in a suit (with collars up) and low-lying hat exiting the house. "May I help you?" Merton asked. The man only replied that he was interested in the vacant room, and that to tell the landlady that he would be back in an hour.

Before Merton could utter a reply, the man was gone. He didn't even see his face; Merton only noticed that his skin was on the dark Caucasian side.

Still not feeling worried, he set out to fix the furnace and returned to their home on the second floor. Hours later, intending to talk to his aunt, he asked the fellow boarders if they had seen her, but all of them replied in the negative. In their search, they happened upon the old woman's corpse; some reports said she was found in the toilet, while others said it was in the vacant room in the attic.

Autopsy reports indicated that aside from being strangled to death with bare hands, she was also sexually assaulted - postmortem.

A Police investigation immediately commenced, but to no avail as the killer remained at large. Two weeks later, on March 2, another victim was killed, this time in San Jose.

Laura Beal, 60, a married woman, and a boarding house manager was nowhere in sight when her husband came home from work. Since he knew that Laura was supposed to be at home, it was strange to find her absent.

Similar to Clara's case, the boarders in the house searched for their landlady until they found her lifeless body in one of the vacant rooms. Laura was naked from her waist down and postmortem exams suggested that she had been raped.

Like Clara, Laura was also strangled, but this time, the killer used the belt of her robe; the belt was so tightly wound around her neck that the skin broke.

The fact that two old women were murdered under similar brutal circumstances caused a period of panic to the residents. The police tried their best to capture the killer, but with not many clues to go by, they were helpless.

The Dark Strangler, as he had been dubbed by the people, went dormant, and soon, he was forgotten by the public. Many thought that he had moved on to another place, but they would soon be proven wrong.

The Horror Continues

Although the Dark Strangler no longer made the front pages of the newspapers, one person still remained engrossed with buying and reading them - the Gorilla Killer himself, Earle Nelson. Apparently, it was in the back pages of the broadsheets where he chose his next victim because that was where the ads for vacant boarding houses were located.

After browsing through the ads, he found a boarding house owned by Lillian St. Mary in San Francisco. Lillian was a widow and she rented rooms out in her home to make extra money for herself and her grown son. So when a large gentleman arrived at her doorstep seeking a room, she gladly welcomed him in - eager to show him the vacant room.

As they trudged up the stairs to the empty second-floor apartment, the gentleman engaged Lillian in small talk, telling her that he wanted an inexpensive room because he was saving for his upcoming marriage. Upon reaching the empty room, Lillian started discussing things like bed sheets, towels, the time for dinner, but she was surprised when she heard the telltale sound of a door being locked.

Just a moment after turning around, the large gentleman was already on her, intent on strangling the life out of her. If Lillian shouted for help, then nobody heard her.

One of Lillian's boarders was innocently making his way to his 3rd-room apartment when he noticed that the vacant room's door on the 2nd floor was open; it was strange, he thought, but it was even stranger when he caught a glimpse of a woman's foot.

Slowly, he walked in and noticed that indeed, a woman was there, laid on the made-up bed - she was also dead.

The body was naked from the waist down, her eyes were bloodshot and bulging her hair was disheveled, but despite the signs of struggle, she was still wearing her glasses. Postmortem reports indicated that she too, was raped after death. Worse, the large man sat on her chest as he strangled her with his bare hands.

Once reported, the police instantly knew that the killer was the same one responsible for Clara Newman and Laura Beal murders. They poured efforts into warning women to never allow any man into their boarding house if they were alone. Authorities thought that if people would be more vigilant, then it would be impossible for the Dark Strangler to continue wreaking havoc.

However, they also knew that the only way to capture him was to have more clues about his identity, and for them to have that, the killer had to make another move: they needed to catch him, but it had to happen before anymore killings.

What they didn't take into consideration, however, was Earle Nelson's tactic: he knew that things were heating up for him in San Francisco, so he decided to create some distance between him and the Police. He found his next haven in Santa Barbara - a resort town, far enough away, that had a lot of boarding houses and where people were complacent about their security.

53 year old Ollie Russel managed a peaceful boarding house in Santa Barbara - unfortunately, the silence would soon be disturbed by the arrival of the Dark Strangler.

On the morning of June 24, 1926, William Franey, a boarder in the house of Mrs. Russel, awoke to the sound of banging on the wall. His first feeling was annoyance; he worked nightshifts so he needed his sleep - he had to tell his noisy neighbors to keep it down.

Intent on calmly conversing with whoever was making the noise, he got out of bed and took a peek on the keyhole of the noisy room. What he saw was a man and woman having sex; the man was large and the woman seemed submissive. When William Franey got a glimpse of the woman, he found it strange that she looked like Mrs. Russel.

He knew for a fact that the landlady was a righteous woman - she would never commit adultery. Confused, Franey set out to find George Russel, Ollie's husband, and together, they went inside the room in question (at this point, the man had already gone).

There, they found that the old landlady had been strangled

to death - the cord wound so tightly that it broke the skin on her neck.

On August of 1926, in Oakland, Stephen Nisbet wondered where his 50 year old wife was - she seemed to have left in the middle of dinner preparations. Stephen was weary, he knew of the horrors happening in the nearby towns to the old landladies and he didn't want his wife to be one of the victims.

His wish for Mary's safety, however, was not granted; for in the second-floor room of their house, Mary laid, half naked and dead.

These murders continued to occur in many different places - Stockton, Oakland, and Portland, Oregon, as well as San Francisco and Santa Barbara. Despite police efforts, Earle Nelson was still able to sneak in and out, deceiving old landladies into believing that he was a harmless tenant-to-be before murdering them and sexually assaulting them.

Somewhere along the line, Earle changed his tactics; his victim became a young woman of 35 years (Beata Withers), and he didn't leave her body in a vacant room - he stuffed it inside a trunk. Since then, Earle's casualties became erratic in characteristics: he still killed old landladies, but he also began killing younger women.

Disposing of the remains also became a creative task for

him. Sometimes he would leave them in vacant rooms, as per his usual MO, but he started to leave them behind other places like the lavatory and behind the furnace. Expert criminologists explained that a change in signature was normal for a serial killer.

According to them, as the murderer became accustomed to his crimes, his shame would develop, hence the need to "cover" the crime by hiding the bodies in certain places.

Earle Nelson in Canada

Like other serial killer stories, the more victims he claimed, the more clues were collected. After his murders in Portland, Earle roamed areas like Philadelphia, New York, Iowa, and Kansas City, before finally deciding that he should cross the American border and head straight to Canada.

There, he rented a house at Smith Street and fooled the old landlady, Catherine Hill, into believing that he was a God-fearing, pleasant man. Unknown to the warm Catherine, the room he rented would become a place of murder.

Lola Cowan was just 14 years old, but already, she had suffered due to poverty. Her father had recently contracted pneumonia, so Lola decided to sell paper flowers door to door to add to her family's meager income. Unfortunately, she was lured in by Earle Nelson, and like so many of his victims, Lola too, was strangled and raped.

She would remain missing until a boarder of Catherine Hill's house found her body in Earle's room, decomposing.

After her, Earle killed a woman named Emily Patterson, but unlike Lola, she was immediately found by her husband, William. At the news of her death, Canadian police instantly knew that the Dark Strangler was in the area, so they made a thorough sweep of every boarding house.

Unlike the previous murders in San Francisco and Santa Barbara, Earle had made a significant number of mistakes, the biggest of which was how his face was often seen (since he rented a room at a boarding house) and leaving Lola Cowan's body in the room he rented (suggesting that he was truly the culprit).

With his face widely known, the police immediately spread the description and every resident was made aware that the fine-looking man was in fact, a murderer.

So when a store owner recognized Earle Nelson as the heartless man who had killed Emily Patterson, his capture became anticlimactic. He went on to effect an escape from the jail in Wakopa, Manitoba not long after he was arrested. However he was recaptured when he boarded the same train as the one carrying a number of Winnipeg policemen.

Foregone Conclusion

In his trial in Manitoba on November 1, 1927, his defense team tried to argue that Earle Nelson was insane, thus, he should not be punished for the murders he had committed. However, the judges were not keen on taking their side, so on January 13, 1928, Earle Nelson was sentenced to death and was hanged at the Vaughan Street Jail in Winnipeg - his total number of victims thought to be more than 21 women.

Chapter 5: Road to Death

If finding a serial killer was already a difficult task for law authorities, how could they describe highway murders? Two words: a nightmare.

Not only can the span of the murders be far and wide, but the clues will be meager: the serial killer will be free to roam the roads, take his prey when no other motorist was around, kill and rape the victim, and dispose of the body in an easy place.

On top of that, since the victims could be found in various places, it would take some time for the police to realize that the different deaths were caused by just one man.

Perhaps, one of the most unforgettable cases of highway killings was that performed by Larry Eyler. His killing spree happened in 4 different states, across 14 counties. It would take 10 corpses before the police conceded that there was a serial killer, and even after having a primary suspect, 13 more would be killed before he was captured.

His Crimes

On October 23, 1982, the mutilated remains of 19 year old

Steven Crockett was found in a cornfield in Kankakee, Illinois, merely 15 miles east of Indiana and 40 miles south of Chicago. One dead body was alarming, but it was not enough to cause a commotion, especially not outside the Kankakee area.

On December 25 of the same year, the body of a second victim, John Johnson was recovered near Lowell, Indiana, some 35 miles away from where Steven's body was found. 25 year old John was reported missing two months prior, from the Chicago's Uptown District where drifters often resided.

Two bodies in two areas were not easy to correlate, especially since the FBI wouldn't computerize information for unsolved murders until June of 1984, so at that point, the police were investigating two separate cases. Unknown to them, the serial killer was a "generous man", so he would soon make more of kills, sending a message to the police that a man like him existed.

On December 28, two new bodies were recovered. One was of 23 year old Steven Agan from Terre Haute, who informed his mother that he was going to catch a movie with the boys, but never returned. Slashed across the throat and stabbed multiple times in the abdomen, his body was dumped in the woods in Newport, in Vermillion

County, Indiana.

His relatives attested that the white socks Steven was wearing did not belong to him. The other body belonged to John Roach, 21 years old, a resident of Indianapolis. Like Steven Agan, John also suffered numerous stab wounds. It was beside Interstate Highway 70 in Putman County where his body was found dumped.

Again, despite the fact that the two murders happened on the same day, Vermillion County and Putman County failed to notice the connection; until they were sent to the same hospital in Bloomington to have the corpses examined by Dr. John Pless (apparently, both counties had no forensic pathologists).

Dr. Pless found it strange that two men were killed under similar circumstances, so he reported the possibility of a serial killer to the police, but they dismissed his claim, even went so far as calling him an "alarmist".

However, when another victim turned up, the authorities in Indianapolis and Chicago were forced to accept the cold fact. The next suspected (as it still wasn't verified) victim was David Block, 22 years old, a recent graduate student from Yale University.

His new Volkswagen was found abandoned at the Tri-State Tollway in Deerfield, Chicago. It would take sometime before David was found in Zionsville, Illinois - his skeletal remains were already badly decomposed.

At this point, all 5 victims were identified as homosexuals and the police in both Indianapolis and Chicago were forced to accept that there may be a serial killer on the loose. The events were reminiscent of the John Wayne Gacy crimes. The only difference was while Gacy tried to conceal his murders, this serial killer was upfront - as if he was taunting not just the police, but also the gay community.

Despite the added effort from the authorities, the homosexual predator continued his killing spree. On March 4, 1983, just outside Danville in Illinois, 27 year old Edgar Underkofler was found dead, stabbed multiple times in various parts of the body, and like Steven Agan, was also wearing an unfamiliar pair of white socks.

After him, Jay Reynolds, 26, was killed on March 21, his body was found in La Fayette County. A little over 2 weeks later, on April 8, several construction workers from Lake County found the body of Gustavo Herrera near the Wisconsin border.

Gustavo had fathered two children, but residents attested that he was also a frequent visitor of gay bars. The serial killer also severed one of his arms and had removed it from the area where he was found.

After them, three more victims were killed - all of whom were homosexuals. The last of the three, Daniel McNeive, 21, was from Henderson County, which didn't have their own pathologist. For the second time, a body was sent to Dr. Pless in Bloomington Hospital. When he reiterated that the crime was performed by familiar hands, the police didn't ignore him.

That time, they finally listened.

Larry Eyler

Accepting that the serial killer would make his next move soon, law enforcement officials from different counties in Indiana started discussing the highway murders. They decided to create a task force named Central Indiana Multi-Agency Investigative Team, headed by Lt. Jerry Campbell from Indianapolis Police Department. Lt. Campbell was assisted by Sgt. Frank Love.

On their second meeting, the task force already had a name for their primary suspect: Larry Eyler, 31 years old. This suspicion was raised by a caller from Indianapolis who pointed to Larry as the man responsible for the attack on Mark Henry, a homosexual from Terre Haute.

According to the informant's story, Larry Eyler gave a lift to Mark, and when the latter refused Larry's sexual advances, the suspect became violent. He stopped his vehicle and forced Mark to lie supine on the bed of the pickup while he handcuffed him.

While Larry was stroking Mark's body with a knife, the victim managed to escape, but when he was caught, Larry stabbed him in the chest, puncturing a lung. After the attack, Mark played dead, and Larry left to get away.

As if he knew how the law would play out, Larry Eyler went to the nearest house and confessed his crime. He then went back to his pickup as he waited for the police to arrest him. The sympathetic judge reduced the previous bond from $50,000 to $10,000 and one of Larry's friends paid the surety of $1,000 for his release. Worse, when Mark Henry was paid with $2,500, he withdrew the case against Larry.

The fact that Larry Eyler was capable of assault against gay men was enough for the police to begin tailing him. They found out that he came from humble beginnings; his parents divorced while he was still a toddler. A high school dropout, Larry was only able to enter college by passing his GED. As it was, he drifted in and out of college from 1974 to 1978, but he eventually quit without a degree.

At the time of the investigation, he lived in Terre Haute with Robert David Little, a university professor. His work in a liquor store was only part-time, but he often went away for some reason unknown to anyone but him.

When Larry murdered Ralph Calise from Chicago, the Illinois police found out that there was an eerie connection between the victims. For an instance, 4 of the victims (Crockett, Herrera, Calise, and Johnson), all lived in the uptown neighborhood of Chicago; in fact, Herrera and Calise were neighbors, only two doors away from each other.

At this point, Illinois police were tipped off that Indiana was also looking for a serial killer with the same MO. The two departments agreed that Larry Eyler could be their man. Together they tailed Larry's every move, but no murder was caught under their watch.

Captured, Freed, and Dead

Larry was spotted in Lowell, where he was pursuing a man to have sex with him in exchange of money. Albeit no evidence was obtained, the Indiana police still arrested Larry on September 30 1983; they also searched his pickup and the home where he lived together with Robert Little. There, they found that several calls had been made to the

Little household from different counties – all areas where the crimes happened. Three other pieces of evidence were recovered, each one consistent with the Ralph Calise murder:

- his boots, which had a plaster cast similar to the crime scene,

- knife with type A (Ralph's blood type), and

- handcuffs which matched Ralph's wounds.

Despite all these, the evidences was still inconclusive, and hence, was not enough. When Larry's lawyer learned of this, he insisted that the police in Indiana had violated his rights when they arrested his client without a proper warrant.

The judge sided with the defense team, and the law authorities who believed that Larry Eyler was the Highway Killer, could only watch as the man was freed.

However, conclusive evidence was found on August 21, 1984, when a janitor in an apartment in West Sherman Street in Chicago found several trash bags containing severed body parts. Upon superficial investigation, one of the tenants reported that a man named Larry Eyler dropped it in the dumpster.

At this point, Larry's conviction was already a foregone

conclusion, but he still fought it. In fact, he said that he was just one half of the Highway Killers - the other one was Robert Little. When the police investigated, however, they found very few clues to connect Robert to any of the murders, so the decision was to convict Larry for the murder and he was sentenced to death on top of serving 15 years in prison.

Larry, however, ran out of time to fulfill the death penalty: on March 6, 1994, he died due from AIDS.

Conclusion

Thank you again for purchasing this book!

Serial killers often act unpredictably - even experts who study them agree that there is no telling how they will react once they have completed a murder.

Many of them become perfectionists, often using the same MO throughout their killing spree and fine tuning it to suit their tastes. Others become braver and take more risks to increase the adrenaline rush.

For others, each murder becomes more brutal than the next, while in some cases, they virtually stop - as if their need to kill had been sated appropriately. All we can say for certain is that it is an area of interest for many people and that many movies, books and television shows have been created in response to this.

What we have discussed in this book are just 5 cases; there are hundreds of known serial killers, and who knows, perhaps, there are still some unidentified ones.

I hope you enjoyed this book, thank you and take care!

Take A Look At Other Books I've Written

Below you'll find some of my other popular books that are popular on Amazon and Kindle as well. You can visit my author page on Amazon to see other work done by me. (Layla Hawkes).

True Paranormal

Serial Killers True Crime

If the links do not work, for whatever reason, you can simply search for these titles on the Amazon website with my name to find them.

Do You Want More Books?

How would you like books arriving in your inbox each week?

They're FREE!

We publish books on all sorts of non-fiction niches and send them to our subscribers each week to spread the love.

All you have to do is sign up and you're good to go!

Just go to the link below, sign up, sit back and wait for your book downloads to arrive.

We couldn't have made it any easier. Enjoy!

www.LibraryBugs.com